I0568878

THE SELF-COACHED ENTREPRENEUR

UNLOCK CLARITY, CONFIDENCE, AND GROWTH
BY ASKING THE RIGHT QUESTIONS

JOHN MEEDZAN

CONTENTS

Copyright © 2025 by The Self-Coach Press

All rights reserved.

No part of this publication may be reproduced, stored in a retrieval system, or transmitted in any form or by any means, electronic, mechanical, photocopying, recording, or otherwise, without the prior written permission of the copyright owner, except for brief quotations used in a review or scholarly work.

ISBN: 979-8-218-67788-6

LCCN: 2025909127

This book is a work of non-fiction. This book is intended for informational purposes only. The author and publisher are not financial, legal, or business advisors, and this publication does not constitute professional advice. Readers are encouraged to seek qualified professionals for specific guidance related to legal, financial, or business decisions.

Printed in the United States of America

First edition

PREFACE: HOW TO USE THIS BOOK

This isn't a book you have to read cover to cover, or finish in one sitting. Instead, think of it as a conversation partner, one that asks you the right questions at the right time. This book will help you unlock clarity, confidence, and growth from within.

Here's how to get the most out of it:

1. Jump Around.
2. Each chapter stands alone. Flip to the topic that speaks to your current challenge.
3. Pause & Reflect.
4. Don't rush. The value comes from reflecting, not racing to the end.
5. Revisit Often.
6. The questions you need answers to, as well as your answers to the questions, will change as you grow. That's the point.
7. Use a Journal.

8. Keep a notebook nearby, or use the margins of this book, to capture insights as they come.
9. Create Your Manifesto.
10. At the end, you'll craft your own set of guiding questions. Let them evolve with you.

Remember:

This isn't about having all the answers.

It's about learning to ask better questions.

FOREWORD

As a founder, coach, and entrepreneur who has led multiple businesses, I've learned that answers don't drive growth; questions do.

The Self-Coached Entrepreneur is not a traditional business guide filled with how-to strategies or step-by-step plans. Instead, it offers self-guided growth through self-reflection. The information contained here is for entrepreneurs who want to build successful businesses without losing themselves. Through powerful questions, storytelling, and coaching prompts, each chapter helps founders pause, realign, and gain clarity. It addresses challenges like procrastination, fear of change, misaligned definitions of success, and burnout.

As an entrepreneur myself, I've always believed in the power of a well-timed quote, the kind that makes you stop, think, and feel seen. Motivational quotes have been a quiet companion throughout my entrepreneurial journey. Taped to my monitor, scribbled in journals, folded into presentations, and emailed to my family, they've helped me push through hard days, reframe challenges, and, most importantly, ask better questions.

That's what led to this book.

I didn't write *The Self-Coached Entrepreneur* because I had all the answers. I wrote it because I was deep in the work of leading a growing company, iLease Management LLC, and I needed clarity, perspective, and space to pause and reflect.

Like most entrepreneurs, I had plans, goals, metrics, and meetings. But underneath it all was a quieter truth: something felt off. Not in the spreadsheets, but in how I was moving through them.

I began to notice that the hardest challenges weren't about logistics, development, or tactics, but about alignment, energy, identity, and momentum.

So, I started writing down questions. These questions helped me pause and really consider what I was doing and where I was going.

This book is a collection of those questions, designed to meet you in the middle of the journey, not the beginning or the end. Each chapter offers a story, a reflection, and a prompt to help you return to what matters. And, yes, you'll find quotes along the way, some that may be familiar, all offered for your pleasure and growth.

As a note of transparency: I wrote this book from my experience launching three startups, currently leading iLease Management LLC, being a college adjunct professor in an MBA and MSIT program, and being a certified agile coach. I used a variety of frameworks and tools, including AI-assisted writing platforms, to help shape and refine this work. The voice, experiences, and questions are fully my own, technology simply helped bring them into focus.

You don't need to read this book in order, and you don't need to finish it in one sitting.

Just let the right question find you when you need it most.

Because a single good question, answered with reflection and truth, can change everything!

—John Meedzan,
Entrepreneur, Agile Coach, and Powerful Question-Asker

INTRODUCTION

Entrepreneurs are overwhelmed with answers but starved for the right questions.

If you're reading this book, chances are you've already created a new product or service. You've launched the business, found the clients, and sent the invoices. Maybe you've even grown a team or hit your first six figures, or your first wall.

But beneath the milestones, you may be wondering:

- Why do I feel stuck, even though things are working?
- Why am I still overthinking every decision?
- Why does this not feel as good as I hoped it would?

The answer, in many cases, isn't more input, another podcast, system, or strategy. What you likely need is a pause and a better question, the kind of question that doesn't just fix a problem, but reveals a pattern; that doesn't just make you smarter, but gives you more clarity.

That's what this book is for.

The Core Belief of This Book

In entrepreneurship, questions will always arise. Developing the ability to navigate them and find the right answers on your own will give you an advantage.

Each chapter in this book offers a short story, practical insight to reflect on and steps you can take to realign and move forward.

Reflect on what's true.
Realign with what matters.
Move forward with clarity.

You don't have to know the answers yet.

But if you're willing to ask better questions, honestly, patiently, and courageously, this book will provide what you need most: *clarity from within*.

Now, you might be wondering, *where do I start?*

The beauty of this book is that you don't have to follow a strict order. Each chapter stands alone, ready to meet you in whatever season of entrepreneurship you're navigating. Still, if you prefer a sense of direction, here's how this journey will unfold:

Your Roadmap to Clarity, Confidence, and Growth

This isn't just a collection of questions, it's a path to realignment, resilience, and sustainable success. The chapters are organized into five key stages that reflect the natural evolution every entrepreneur may face:

1. See Yourself Clearly
   The Power of Entrepreneurial Awareness

   Reconnect with your purpose, redefine success on your terms, and recognize the growth you've already achieved.

2. The Courage to Evolve
   Moving Beyond Fear in Business

   Identify where things are holding you back, whether it's procrastination, limiting beliefs, or resistance to change, and discover how to move forward intentionally.

3. Lead in Alignment
   Building a Business True to You

   Shift from reactive decisions to purposeful leadership by aligning your actions with your values and vision.

4. Work Smarter, Not Harder
   Creating Sustainable Success

   Simplify your processes, honor your energy, and design a business that supports both growth and well-being.

5. Keep Moving Forward

The Mindset of Sustainable Growth

Learn how to maintain momentum by using intentional questions as your compass, ensuring you grow without losing yourself along the way.

You can start at the beginning, flip to the section that resonates most today, or revisit chapters as new challenges arise. There's no wrong way to navigate this book, only the way that keeps you connected to what matters.

So, take a breath, and open to where you feel called.

"**Self-reflection entails asking yourself questions about your values, assessing your strengths and failures, thinking about your perceptions and interactions with others, and imagining where you want to take your life in the future.**"

—ROBERT L. ROSEN

Let's begin with a single, better question.

PART 1
SEE YOURSELF CLEARLY
THE POWER OF ENTREPRENEURIAL AWARENESS

ONE
DON'T LOSE SIGHT OF YOUR WHY

"People don't buy what you do; they buy why you do it."

— SIMON SINEK, *START WITH WHY*

The Presentation That Didn't Land

Bridget stood in front of a group of angel investors, her slide deck polished to perfection. Her startup, a workplace wellness platform, had decent traction. The numbers were solid, and her pitch was tight.

But as she wrapped up her presentation, one of the investors leaned forward and asked a question that caught her off guard:

"I get what it does. But why are *you* building this?"

Bridget blinked, and her throat tightened. She hadn't expected *that* question. She gave a quick answer about market opportunity and growing trends, but the energy in the room had shifted.

After the meeting, her advisor pulled her aside. "You know what I didn't hear?" he said. "You, your heart, your story. The part about what you're building and why it truly matters."

Bridget had built a great product. But she'd forgotten to stay connected to the reason she started building it in the first place.

Let's Reflect on This

You risk burnout if you disconnect from purpose. Without meaning, momentum fades.

As entrepreneurs, we're taught to focus on what we're building, our product, our pitch, our funnel, our forecast.

But if we don't stay connected to *why it matters to us*, we lose our anchor. We start chasing validation instead of vision. We perform success instead of experiencing it. And worst of all, we burn out trying to build something that doesn't feed us anymore.

Your venture doesn't just need a market fit. It needs a *meaning that fits* with you.

That doesn't mean you need a dramatic origin story. It just means your business needs to stay connected to you.

Because when you remember *why* it matters, you make better decisions. You communicate with more clarity. And you can pivot without losing your purpose.

The question: **What am I building, and why does it matter to me?** is your anchor in the noise.

Realign & Move Forward

Let's forget the metrics for a moment and go deeper, to the part of you that started this in the first place.

1. If I asked you to describe what you're building, not in features or deliverables, but in meaning, what would you say?
2. Who or what is this business really for? Is that still true today?
3. When you picture your business *working beautifully*, how does it feel, not just for your clients, but for you?
4. What's something you've been building out of habit, obligation, or momentum, but not joy?
5. If you could make one small shift to reconnect with why these matter to you, what would that be?

Don't Lose Sight of Your Why

You started this for a reason, don't lose that thread. If you've drifted, that's okay. Just come back to what still feels true and build from there.

Action: Write down your original *why* and circle the part that still resonates.

TWO
DEFINING YOUR SUCCESS

"A value is a way of being or believing that we hold most important. Living into our values means that we do more than profess our values, we practice them."

—BRENÉ BROWN, *DARE TO LEAD*

Winning the Wrong Game

Thomas scrolled through his feed after a long day. Another funding announcement, another founder hitting seven figures. Another TEDx speaker with a neon-lit personal brand and a hundred thousand followers.

He looked up from his phone and stared at the whiteboard in his office, half doodles, half goals. They used to excite him. But lately, they just made him tired.

The funny thing was his business *wasn't* failing. Revenue was steady. Clients were happy. He had finally hired two part-time contractors to help with the workload. But it didn't feel like enough.

He couldn't shake the feeling that he was behind, that he should be doing *more*, scaling faster, hustling harder.

At dinner that night, his partner asked a simple question:

"Hey, what would 'enough' actually look like to you?"

Thomas didn't have an answer.

He realized he'd been chasing someone else's version of success, loud, shiny, external, without ever defining his own.

It wasn't that he *couldn't* win the game. It's that he'd never stopped to ask *if he even wanted to play it.*

Let's Reflect on This

When you compare, you lose sight of what truly matters to you. In entrepreneurship, success is often mistaken for a formula, focused on numbers, not on meaning.

But rarely do we ask: *Is this even what I want?*

When you don't define success for yourself, you default to chasing other people's metrics. And the more you chase, the more you lose connection with your own voice.

That disconnection shows up as burnout, boredom, restlessness, even resentment toward a business that's *technically working*.

Clarity doesn't come from more input. It comes from *pausing long enough to listen to what you really want*.

This question: **What does success look like** *for me*? is an invitation to stop performing and start defining.

Realign & Move Forward

Let's take a step back from the numbers for a second. Not because they don't matter, but because they don't matter *more* than how it feels to live with them.

1. If you had no one to impress, no social media, no industry benchmarks, no outside pressure, what would success honestly look and feel like to you?
2. What version of success have you been chasing that doesn't actually belong to you?
3. How do you want to feel in your business, not just once you "make it," but as you go?
4. Where are you tolerating misalignment in the name of productivity or growth?
5. What would shift if your definition of success prioritized *sustainability, joy, and impact* over optics and output?

Defining Your Success

Success isn't one-size-fits-all. If the version you're chasing feels heavy or hollow, it might not be yours. Redefine it, on your terms.

Action: Define success in one sentence, based on how you want your business to *feel*, not just perform.

THREE
RECOGNIZE AND CELEBRATE HOW YOU'VE GROWN

"We do not learn from experience . . . we learn from reflecting on experience."

—JOHN DEWEY

The Blind Spot Called *Progress*

Leah was preparing for a quarterly planning retreat, new goals, new strategy, new revenue targets.

But as she worked through the pre-retreat worksheets, one prompt made her freeze: "List 3 things you're proud of from the last quarter."

She stared at the page.

She had launched a new service, hired her first part-time assistant, and closed her biggest client deal to date.

And yet . . . she hadn't paused to *feel* any of it.

All of it had been quickly followed by, *"Okay, what's next?"*

That night, she pulled out an old notebook from the year before. Her handwriting was messier, her planning less confident. Her goals, then very intimidating to her, were now her new normal.

She hadn't just grown her business; she had grown *herself*.

And the only reason she hadn't noticed?

She never gave herself time to look back.

Let's Reflect on This

Entrepreneurs are always chasing the next level but rarely stop to see how far they've already come.

We default to:

- "What's next?"
- "What's not working?"
- "What still needs to be fixed?"

But here's the truth: if you don't witness your growth, you'll keep chasing progress you've already made, without ever feeling it.

Growth that isn't acknowledged doesn't integrate. It stays out of reach, even when it's already yours.

This question: **How have I grown, and do I give myself credit?** isn't about celebration for celebration's sake.

It's about reconnecting with how far you've come, so you don't forget who you've already become.

Realign & Move Forward

Let's step out of the planning mindset. Let's look backward, not with judgment, but with kindness.

1. In the past 6–12 months, what can you do now that you once doubted, feared, or avoided?
2. What situations used to drain you, scare you, or throw you off track, that you now navigate with more clarity?
3. Where have you become more confident, more honest, or more fully *yourself* in your work?
4. What success, shift, or boundary have you skipped over instead of honoring?
5. If you let yourself feel proud, not for being perfect, but for being *present* in your growth, what would that feel like?

Recognize and Celebrate How You've Grown

You've come further than you think. But if you never pause to witness it, you'll miss the progress you've already earned.

Action: List three ways you've grown in the last six months, and give yourself credit out loud.

FOUR

TRUST AND FOLLOW YOUR OWN ADVICE

"Trust thyself: every heart vibrates to that iron string."

—RALPH WALDO EMERSON

The Advice Loop

Lyn was brilliant at helping other people get unstuck.

As a strategist and coach, she could cut through the noise in minutes. When clients wavered, she reminded them of their core values. When they got lost in options, she brought them back to purpose.

But when it came to her own business, Lyn felt stuck.

She'd been sitting on a decision for weeks, whether to

sunset one of her legacy programs. It still brought in revenue, but it no longer aligned with her focus or energy.

She made pros and cons lists, asked her mastermind group, meditated, and waited for clarity.

Finally, a friend asked, "If a client brought this to you, same facts, same feelings, what would you tell them?"

Lyn didn't hesitate. "I'd tell them to let it go. It's not aligned anymore."

Her friend smiled. "Then why are you still holding on?"

Lyn sighed. "Because I'm afraid. And because when it's me, I forget I already know what to do."

Let's Reflect on This

You already know more than you give yourself credit for.

As entrepreneurs, we often give better advice than we're willing to follow.

This is not because we're hypocrites, but because we carry more emotion, fear, and responsibility in our own decisions.

But self-trust is a muscle, and sometimes the clearest way to build it is to ask, "If someone I respected was in my shoes, what would I say to them?"

That one question: *Would I follow my own advice?* quietly demands honesty.

It reconnects you to your core wisdom. And it reminds you that the voice of clarity isn't out there, it's in you. You just need to trust it again.

THE SELF-COACHED ENTREPRENEUR

Realign & Move Forward

Let's take the pressure off the outcome. Let's just notice what you already know.

1. Think of a decision you've been avoiding or obsessing over. What advice would you give to a friend in your exact position?
2. How would that advice sound if it came from the most grounded, wise version of you?
3. What's stopping you from taking that same advice for yourself?
4. What fear, doubt, or pressure is creating static in your ability to trust what you know?
5. What would shift if you moved forward, not from certainty, but from trust in your own inner compass?

Trust and Follow Your Own Advice

You give wise counsel, don't forget you're allowed to receive it too. Self-trust grows when you stop outsourcing your knowing.

Action: Ask yourself, "What would I say to a friend in this exact situation?"... then take your own advice.

PART 2
THE COURAGE TO EVOLVE

THE COURAGE TO EVOLVE: MOVING BEYOND FEAR IN BUSINESS

FIVE
MOVING PAST PROCRASTINATION

"The moment you have an instinct to act on a goal you must 5-4-3-2-1 and physically move or your brain will stop you."

—MEL ROBBINS, *THE 5 SECOND RULE*

The Invisible Weight

For weeks, Joe had been avoiding sending the beta to three VIP clients. He knew the product wasn't perfect, but it was ready, and his team was waiting for the green light.

But every time he opened the email draft, his stomach twisted. What if they hate it? What if they say nothing at all? What if this proves I'm not ready?

He found reasons to delay. He updated the onboarding copy. He asked his developer to tweak one more setting. He changed the subject line, twice.

When his advisor called to check in, Joe admitted, "I don't know why I keep putting this off. I *want* it out there, but I keep stalling."

His advisor replied, "You're not lazy, you're scared. You keep delaying to protect yourself from the unknown."

Joe hadn't thought of it that way.

The problem wasn't that the beta wasn't ready to send, it was **what sending it represented**: visibility, vulnerability, and the possibility of not measuring up.

Let's Reflect on This

Delays often sound logical, but underneath, they're driven by fear.

Entrepreneurs are great at rationalizing delays:

- "It's not quite ready yet."
- "I just need a few more hours to tweak it."
- "The timing doesn't feel right."

And while sometimes that's true, often it's not the *task* that's the problem, but the *emotions underneath it*.

Procrastination becomes a coping mechanism for:

- Fear of rejection or failure
- Fear of being seen and still not feeling enough

- Fear of committing to something that makes you vulnerable

This question: *Why do I keep putting this off?* helps surface what's real:

- Is this about timing?
- Or could it be something deeper, a tension I haven't fully acknowledged?
- And if that's true, what would it take to face it with honesty instead of avoidance?

Once you see the fear clearly, it stops hiding behind your to-do list.

Realign & Move Forward

Let's look at what's going on, not to criticize, but to understand.

1. What's the task, message, or decision you've been avoiding, despite knowing it matters?
2. If you were to be completely honest, what are you afraid might happen *after* you follow through?
3. What emotion are you avoiding, failure, judgment, not feeling ready?
4. What story are you telling yourself about what this delay is "protecting" you from?
5. If we reframed the risk as *a signal that something matters*, what would it mean to take one courageous step forward?

Moving Past Procrastination

Procrastination is often self-protection, not a flaw. You're not lazy, you're protecting yourself.

Action: Identify one task you've been avoiding and write down the emotion underneath it.

SIX

BREAK FREE FROM LIMITING BELIEFS

"No matter what your ability is, effort is what ignites that ability and turns it into accomplishment."

—CAROL S. DWECK, *MINDSET*

The Unspoken Ceiling

Mary Kate had built a thriving consulting firm over the last two years. She had steady clients, a strong referral network, and glowing feedback. On the surface, things were going well. But deep down, something felt off.

She was booked solid, working long hours, and saying yes to everything. But her revenue had flatlined.

Every few weeks, she'd open her rate card to make

updates. "I should raise my prices," she'd tell herself. Her services had grown more valuable, as her clients were getting real results.

But then came the thought:

- What if they walk away?
- What if I raise my rates and lose half my clients?
- What if this decision shrinks my pipeline and hurts my bottom line?

Mary Kate wasn't just afraid of rejection. She was afraid of *loss*, loss of income, loss of trust, loss of momentum.

She was afraid that one bold move might unravel the stable, but increasingly strained, business she had built.

One afternoon, after finishing a strategy session for a new client, one that she knew deep down she had underpriced, she brought it up to her colleague, Jonah.

"I've been thinking about raising my rates," she said. "But I'm worried. If even a few clients drop off, that's a big hit to my bottom line."

Jonah nodded. "That's a real concern," he said. "But let me ask you something. If you keep charging what you're charging now and keep working this much, how long can you sustain it?"

She hesitated. "Honestly? Not long."

"Then maybe the question isn't, 'Can I afford to raise my rates?'" Jonah said. "It's, 'Can I afford not to?'"

That night, Mary Kate sat down with her notebook and wrote out the thoughts looping in her head:

"If I charge more, they'll think I'm greedy."

"People like me don't earn that kind of money."

"What if no one thinks I'm worth it?"

She stared at the page and felt a pit in her stomach, not because the thoughts were new, but because they were *familiar*.

She had built a business on skill, heart, and hustle. But underneath it all was a belief:

You're only valuable if you're affordable.

And just like that, she saw it clearly. She wasn't just protecting her bottom line, she was protecting a story she didn't believe in anymore.

Let's Reflect on This

The beliefs that hold us back are rarely loud. They're quiet, practiced, and disguised as truth.

Entrepreneurs don't just carry strategies, they carry stories:

- Stories about money, worth, visibility, risk, and identity.
- Stories that were shaped by early experiences, past failures, or people who meant well but didn't understand what we were trying to build.

These stories become beliefs. These beliefs shape what we say yes to, what we charge, what we hide, and how long we wait before stepping into our next level. Sometimes, we don't need a new business model. We need a new belief.

This question: **What belief is holding me back?** is an invitation to step out from under the ceiling you didn't realize was there.

Realign & Move Forward

Let's consider this. Gently. You don't need to force anything. Just be honest with yourself.

1. Think of something in your business that feels stuck. If we were talking face-to-face, what would you say is really behind that block?
2. What's a belief you've carried about success, worth, money, or visibility that might no longer be true?
3. Where did that belief come from? Is it something you learned, or something you chose?
4. What's the cost of continuing to act from that belief?
5. If you could try on a new belief, just for a week, what would you want it to be?

Break Free from Limiting Beliefs

Sometimes it's not your strategy that needs upgrading, it's your story. Try on a new belief that supports who you're becoming.

Action: Replace one limiting belief with a more honest one, and practice living from it for the next 7 days.

SEVEN
KNOWING WHEN IT'S TIME TO PIVOT

"The art of life is a constant readjustment to our surroundings."

—KAKUZŌ OKAKURA

The Moment He Didn't Listen

In the early 1990s, before broadband internet, video streaming, and online applications were the norm, John founded a company to solve a real problem for colleges: how to get their marketing materials, campus videos, and student application forms into the hands of prospective students in a more compelling way than paper mailings.

The solution? Put it all on a CD-ROM. The product was called CD2000.

At the time, it was a breakthrough. CD-ROMs could deliver rich multimedia experiences that dial-up internet simply couldn't handle. Schools loved it, and John's company gained traction. He believed he had found a winning edge.

Still, something nagged at him. Was the CD-ROM the future . . . or just a temporary bridge?

To get clarity, he reached out to his old college friend, Mike. Mike was now a senior executive at a major Boston-based marketing firm, soon to be its CEO.

John walked him through the product and the vision: fast access, full video, user-friendly experience. "The internet can't do this yet," he explained. "It's too slow. It's not ready for this kind of content."

Mike paused. He was thoughtful, not dismissive.

"I think it's a smart product," he said. "But I'll be honest, our firm is moving everything to the internet. That's where we're going. So let me ask you something, John, **if the technology changes faster than your model does, what's your plan?**"

John blinked. Then he answered with confidence, talking through the advantages of offline access, the reliability of the CD-ROM, and the immediate user experience.

But internally, he froze.

Mike hadn't challenged the product, he had challenged the *strategic focus.*

And John wasn't ready to answer that.

Really considering Mike's question would've meant unpacking his entire roadmap. It would have meant rethinking what he built, why, and what came next. And at that moment, that kind of shift felt too big. Too destabilizing. Too soon.

So he stayed the course.

Eventually, the internet caught up. Broadband made it easy to stream, download, and browse, and CD2000's advantage disappeared. The product didn't fail overnight. It just stopped being necessary.

Looking back, the moment that could've changed everything wasn't a product failure, it was a moment of ignored insight. John had been asked a better question.

He just wasn't ready to let it change him.

Let's Reflect on This

Pivots feel personal because identity is attached to the plan.

Entrepreneurs often fuse their self-worth with the direction they started in. And even when the data changes, the market shifts, or someone you trust offers a glimpse of the future, it's hard to let go.

Why?

Because change means admitting that what once worked . . . might not anymore.

But that's not failure. That's *evolution*.

The real danger isn't being wrong about the past, it's being unwilling to be right about the present.

Sometimes holding on is what holds you back. Staying loyal to your original idea can sometimes mean betraying your future.

This question: **Is it time to shift, even if it changes everything?** isn't about panic or pressure. It's about your ability and courage to respond when the world moves.

Realign & Move Forward

Let's take the pressure off. You don't need to burn everything down. You just need to get honest.

1. What part of your business feels heavy, outdated, or misaligned, even if it still "works"?
2. What feedback, data, or instinct have you been quietly ignoring?
3. If you started this business today, from scratch, would you build the same thing?
4. What belief or identity might you have to release in order to pivot?
5. What would become possible if you stopped defending the plan, and started listening to what wants to happen next?

Knowing When It's Time to Pivot

What once served you might now be holding you back. Pivoting isn't quitting, it's listening.

Action: Ask yourself: "If I started fresh today, would I build this the same way?" Let the answer guide you.

EIGHT

LET GO TO MAKE SPACE FOR GROWTH

"The secret of change is to focus all of your energy not on fighting the old, but on building the new."

—SOCRATES

The Offer That Had Expired

Andy had built his business around a signature offer, a six-week group program that had once been a breakthrough for both his clients and his revenue. It was clean. Scalable. Profitable.

But lately, every time he launched it, it took more effort to fill. On top of that, he felt disconnected while delivering it. The testimonials were still good, but the spark was gone.

During a team check-in, one of his contractors asked if he planned to update the curriculum again.

Andy paused. "I think I've been updating something I don't even want to keep."

Later that week, during a long walk, the thought returned to Andy: This offer served its purpose. It gave me traction. It taught me so much. But it's done.

That thought, though quiet, felt like relief.

He realized he wasn't tired because he was scaling.

He was tired because he was dragging something behind him that no longer fit.

Letting go wasn't easy. But it made room for what was next.

And when he did let go, clarity rushed in.

Let's Reflect on This

Most things in your business won't last forever. They're not supposed to.

But we often hold on too long, because the offer worked once, or the identity got applause, or the partnership made us feel safe.

When something has run its course, letting go isn't wasteful, it's strategic.

It frees your energy, reclaims your focus, honors your growth.

The hard part is grieving what worked.

But it is so freeing to open space for what's next. This question: **What's asking to be let go?** isn't about abandoning things impulsively.

It's about recognizing when something no longer fits, and being brave enough to say so.

Realign & Move Forward

Let's take a breath and hold space for something to be over, even if it once felt essential.

1. What part of your business feels heavy, misaligned, or no longer fulfilling, even if it still works on the surface?
2. What have you been maintaining out of obligation, fear, or nostalgia?
3. What emotion comes up when you imagine letting it go, relief, sadness, fear, clarity?
4. What is this thing, offer, identity, commitment—costing you to keep?
5. What would you gain if you released it with honesty and grace?

Let Go to Make Space for Growth

Not everything is meant to go with you. When something feels done, it probably is.

Action: Name one offer, habit, or belief you've outgrown, and write down what it's costing you to keep it.

PART 3
LEAD IN ALIGNMENT

LEAD IN ALIGNMENT: BUILDING A BUSINESS TRUE TO YOU

NINE

MAKING PURPOSE-DRIVEN DECISIONS

"The world makes much less sense than you think. The coherence comes mostly from the way your mind works."

—DANIEL KAHNEMAN, *THINKING, FAST AND SLOW*

The Rush to React

Julia was facing pressure on all sides. A competitor had just launched a flashier version of a similar service. Her inbox was full of messages asking if she planned to match the pricing. One of her investors had casually asked, "What's your response strategy?"

So, she did what many founders do: she sprang into action.

She called her dev team to brainstorm features. She made a list of quick wins for marketing. She even started rewriting her pricing model, slashing rates to stay competitive.

But nothing about it felt right. Her chest was tight. Her focus was scattered. Her calendar looked full, but her gut told her she was building in the wrong direction.

Over lunch, a mentor asked her one question: "Are you making these decisions because they feel true, or because you feel afraid?"

Julia paused. She realized she hadn't *chosen* her next move, she was reacting to pressure, fear, and the imagined judgment of people who weren't even her customers.

She had confused *urgency* with *clarity*.

Let's Reflect on This

Anxiety creates a false sense of momentum.

As entrepreneurs, it's easy to get caught up in pressure, market shifts, expectations, comparison, fear of missing out. But not all movement is progress.

Sometimes, we're moving fast because we're uncomfortable sitting still. Sometimes, we're fixing problems that don't exist. Sometimes, we're saying yes because we're afraid of what "no" might cost.

The antidote isn't inaction, it's *alignment*.

Alignment doesn't mean certainty. It means the decision feels like it comes from your values, not your fear.

This question: **Am I making this decision from alignment or anxiety?** asks you to pause before you pivot, launch, quit, or double down.

The action you ultimately choose to take may be the same, but the *outcome* often depends on the energy behind it.

Realign & Move Forward

Let's take a breath. You don't have to solve everything right now. Let's just check in.

1. What decision are you currently facing that feels rushed, tense, or confusing?
2. What emotion is leading the charge, urgency, fear, control, clarity, peace?
3. If you paused for 24 hours and came back to this, what might change?
4. If this decision were coming from alignment, your values, your long-game vision, how would it feel?
5. What would shift if you permitted yourself to move slower . . . and deeper?

Making Purpose-Driven Decisions

Pressure can push you fast, but fast doesn't always mean forward. Lead from alignment, not urgency.

Action: Delay your next big decision by 24 hours. Use the time to reconnect with your long-game vision.

TEN
LEAD WITH CONFIDENCE, NOT VALIDATION

"He who trims himself to suit everyone will soon whittle himself away."

—RAYMOND HULL

The Shiny Offer

Nancy had finally hit a groove in her business. Her coaching practice had grown steadily, her clients were getting real results, and her calendar was filling up with the right kind of work.

Then came the opportunity: a speaking engagement for a major conference. There would be big names, press coverage, and exposure.

The catch? It wasn't aligned with her core audience. It

would require a new set of slides, a new story, and an entirely new set of talking points she didn't feel connected to anymore.

But it was *impressive*, and that's what made it hard to say no. She accepted the invitation, convinced that it would raise her visibility. However, in the following weeks, she found herself overwhelmed, resentful, and oddly disconnected from her business. She didn't feel more successful. She felt scattered.

Over dinner with a friend, she finally said it out loud: "I think I did this to prove I'm legit."

Her friend smiled gently. "You've been acting like you still have something to prove. What if you don't?"

Nancy sat with that. She realized she was building something true, but still reaching for recognition that no longer aligned with who she was becoming.

Let's Reflect on This

You don't have to earn your place with performance. The need to prove is a form of fear dressed as ambition.

Entrepreneurs often start with a vision, but somewhere along the way, it can get hijacked by the need to *be seen, validated,* or *approved of.* We chase clients who don't fit, say yes to partnerships that aren't aligned, and overdeliver to prove we're worth it.

Sometimes we're not building for the future, we're building to silence the past.

But here's the truth: the need to prove something rarely comes from your most aligned self. It comes from the version of you still waiting for permission.

This question: **Where am I trying to prove something?**

is a mirror. It helps you reclaim energy, reshape your decisions, and rebuild your business *from confidence, not the need for recognition.*

Realign & Move Forward

Let's be honest for a moment. You don't need to shame yourself for being ambitious. You just need to know what's fueling it.

1. What recent decision or offer have you said yes to because it looked impressive, not because it felt aligned?
2. Who are you trying to impress or prove something to? (Be honest, it could be someone else . . . or a past version of yourself.)
3. What are you hoping your success will finally prove to others, or to you?
4. What would change if you no longer needed to be seen a certain way?
5. What does it look like to build from self-trust, not self-doubt disguised as drive?

Lead with Confidence, Not Validation

You don't need to prove your worth to claim your space. Build from confidence, not the need for recognition.

Action: Audit your last "yes." Did it come from alignment or a need to be seen?

ELEVEN

DESIGN A BUSINESS WHERE YOU THRIVE

"The energy of the mind is the essence of life."

—ARISTOTLE

The Schedule That Looked Right but Felt Wrong

Lena's calendar was full, and that was the problem.

She had built a coaching business that was technically thriving. Every slot was booked. She had recurring revenue. Her systems were clean.

But each day, she felt more tired, not the kind of tired that rest fixes, but the kind that slowly erodes motivation.

During a mid-week coffee with her accountability group, one of her peers asked, "What's something in your business that feels good lately?"

Lena went quiet. After a pause, she admitted, "I love writing and hosting small-group intensives. But honestly . . . most of my one-on-one calls drain me."

Her friend leaned in. "So why are you doing so many of them?"

Lena looked down at her latte. "Because I thought that's what I was *supposed* to do to be successful."

That night, Lena went home and opened a blank page. She wrote two columns: "What gives me energy" and "What drains me." What she saw was undeniable.

She hadn't created a business around her strengths.

She'd created one around what she thought success was supposed to look like.

Let's Reflect on This

Your energy is a form of data. But most entrepreneurs ignore it.

We optimize for efficiency, profit, and growth, but rarely for joy. Over time, we convince ourselves that dragging through the day is just part of the job.

But here's the truth: When something drains you consistently, it's trying to teach you something.

And when something energizes you, it's pointing to your next evolution.

This question: **What's draining me, and what's energizing me?** is about paying attention to your internal dashboard.

Because your best strategy isn't just the one that works. It's the one you can *sustain*.

Realign & Move Forward

Let's pause. No guilt. No "shoulds." Just honesty.

1. If I asked you to list the top 5 things you do in a typical work week . . . which ones give you energy, and which ones quietly steal it?
2. What patterns do you notice between what drains you and what lights you up?
3. What tasks or responsibilities are you holding onto out of habit, fear, or obligation?
4. What part of your work do you miss, because it made you feel *most like yourself*?
5. What's one small shift you can make this week to reclaim some energy, by saying no, saying yes, or making space?

Design a Business Where You Thrive

Energy is feedback. If something drains you, it's trying to tell you something.

Action: List what energized versus drained you this week, and make one shift that energized you.

TWELVE
ALIGN YOUR BRAND WITH WHO YOU ARE

"In every line of copy we write, we're either serving the customer's story or descending into confusion; we're either making music or making noise."

—DONALD MILLER, *BUILDING A STORYBRAND*

The Personal Brand That Didn't Fit Anymore

Monica had grown her audience steadily over three years. Her posts were polished. Her newsletter went out every Monday. Her brand voice was upbeat, clever, and full of productivity tips.

But behind the scenes, Monica was tired, not from the workload, but from the disconnect.

She no longer resonated with the persona she had built,

and she wasn't obsessed with productivity hacks anymore. She was thinking more about depth, focus, leadership, and the emotional side of entrepreneurship. But she kept posting the same kind of content because it was what people expected.

One day, during a podcast interview, the host asked,

"What do you want to be known for, ten years from now?"

Monica hesitated before giving a smart-sounding answer. In that moment, deep down, she realized she didn't want to be known as the "systems and hacks" expert anymore.

She wanted to be known for helping people create businesses that *felt* as good as they looked.

And her content needed to catch up to that.

She didn't need more visibility.

She needed **aligned visibility**.

Let's Reflect on This

You're already becoming known for something. The only question is, what?

In a world where exposure is currency, it's easy to build a brand that gets attention . . . but not alignment. And over time, the gap between who you *are* and how you show up creates friction, both for you and your audience.

A reputation that aligns with who you really are is not a marketing strategy, it's the result of consistent, authentic choices.

This question: **What do I want to be known for?** helps you pause and take the time to define your impact *on purpose*, not by accident.

Realign & Move Forward

Let's drop the pressure to impress. Let's get curious about what *matters most* to be known for, not just what's marketable.

1. If your next 90 days of visibility determined your long-term reputation, what would people assume you care about most?
2. Does that match what you actually want to be known for?
3. What part of your message, brand, or presence feels outdated, but you've kept it going because "it still works"?
4. What values, skills, or perspective do you want your work to amplify now?
5. What's one small way you can begin to show up today as the future version of what you want to be known for?

Align Your Brand with Who You Are

You've evolved, let your brand evolve with you. Show up as the version of you that feels honest now.

Action: Update one part of your public-facing brand (bio, post, pitch) to reflect who you are today.

PART 4

WORK SMARTER, NOT HARDER

CREATE SUSTAINABLE SUCCESS WITHOUT THE OVERWHELM

THIRTEEN

GET TO THE ROOT OF THE PROBLEM

"The Five Whys is another lean manufacturing tool pioneered by Toyota. When faced with a problem, the first answer will likely be superficial and fail to address the root cause."

—EDIFY.ME

Uncovering What Was Really Blocking Sam

Sam had recently launched a new website for his business. It looked great. The copy was clean, the layout was professional, and the funnel had all the right steps.

But it wasn't working.

Visitors weren't booking calls. The conversion rate was

flat. And Sam, frustrated, found himself questioning every-thing. He brought this issue up during a coaching session.

"I think I need a new web designer and a full redesign," he said.

His coach paused and then said: "Let's back up. Can we try something? Let's use the Five Whys, where we just ask 'why?' until we get closer to the real problem."

Sam nodded.

1. **Why isn't the website working?** "Because people aren't booking discovery calls."
2. **Why aren't they booking calls?** "I don't think they feel a connection to what I'm offering."
3. **Why might they feel disconnected?** "Maybe because the way I talk about my work on the site doesn't match how I talk about it now."
4. **Why doesn't it match how you talk about it now?** "Because I've changed. My message has evolved. But my website still reflects the old version of me."
5. **Why haven't you updated it to reflect who you are now?** "Honestly? I'm scared to let go of that version. It feels like leaving behind what I worked so hard to build."

That's when it hit him.

The problem wasn't his homepage. It was his hesitance to step into a new identity.

The disconnect wasn't between James and his audience, it was between *Sam and himself.*

He didn't need a redesign.

He needed realignment.

Let's Reflect on This

Entrepreneurs often fix symptoms instead of addressing the source of the issue.

When something feels off in your business, the first instinct is often to adjust a strategy: rework the offer, redesign the brand, and relaunch the campaign.

But the root cause is rarely just technical. It's emotional, identity-driven, a reflection of something unspoken trying to surface.

When what you're doing doesn't feel right, don't reach for a new tool. Reach for a better question.

This chapter's question: **What is this really about?** isn't always easy. But it's almost always necessary.

It moves you past surface tweaks and into meaningful change.

Realign & Move Forward

Let's slow it down. There's nothing wrong with fixing what's visible, but what if we went a level deeper?

1. What's one challenge or frustration in your business that you keep trying to "solve," but it never quite clicks?
2. What do you *say* the problem is?
3. Now ask yourself, "Why?"

4. And then ask, "Why?" again.
5. And again.
6. Ask why five times or more, until you feel the real answer land.
7. What story or pattern is repeating, and why might it be easier to stay there?
8. What do you *already know*, deep down, that you haven't yet said out loud?
9. What becomes possible when you finally name what this is *really* about?

Get to the Root of the Problem

Surface fixes don't always fix the problem. Get honest about what's really in the way.

Action: Use the "Five Whys" method on one business challenge. Question "Why?" until you hit something real.

Sit with what you find, not to fix, but to understand.

Your fifth answer is often something you've been avoiding, not because it's wrong, but because it asks you to grow.

FOURTEEN

SIMPLIFY YOUR WORK WITHOUT LOSING IMPACT

"Essentialism is not about how to get more things done; it's about how to get the right things done."

—GREG MCKEOWN, *ESSENTIALISM*

The Hustle That Stopped Feeling Smart

Victor had always been a builder. He liked motion, action, hustle.

He'd built his marketing agency from scratch, working early mornings and late nights and taking big risks.

But something had shifted.

Now that the agency was running well, the hustle didn't feel satisfying. It felt automatic. He was still adding projects, still chasing new channels, still trying to prove something, but he wasn't sure what.

One night, while reviewing his project tracker, his partner looked over his shoulder. "You've got six campaigns launching in the next three weeks," she said. "Why?"

Victor blinked. "Because . . . that's what growth looks like?"

His partner didn't push back, just nodded and asked, "What would this look like if you didn't make it hard?"

The question hit him in the chest.

He realized that somewhere along the way, difficulty had become a proxy for value. He trusted things more when they were heavy. He associated complexity with legitimacy.

But complexity had stopped working.

And what he really wanted was progress that felt *honest, simple, and smart.*

Let's Reflect on This

Many entrepreneurs confuse ease with weakness.

But ease isn't laziness or giving up. Ease is flow, clarity, breathing room. It's doing things the way that's *right for you*, not the hardest way possible.

We glorify the grind because we don't always trust that ease can deliver real results. But some of your best decisions will come when you stop asking, "How can I do more?" and start asking, "How can I make this work better, with less resistance?"

This question: **How could this be easier without losing**

impact? isn't about shortcuts. It's about sustainability and building something you don't need to recover from.

Realign & Move Forward

Let's remove the assumption that everything worth doing has to feel heavy.

1. Where in your business are you making something that could be simple, hard?
2. What do you believe about ease? Is it risky? Unreliable? Undeserved?
3. What process, offer, or relationship have you been "white knuckling" just to hold it together?
4. What part of your week would benefit from more grace, more space, or more trust?
5. If you stopped proving and started designing . . . what would feel like *just enough* effort?

Simplify Your Work without Losing Impact

Hard doesn't always mean better. Let ease become a strategy, not a luxury.

Action: Choose one area to simplify this week, your calendar, offer, or onboarding flow.

FIFTEEN
WEARING MULTIPLE HATS

"You can do anything, but not everything."

—DAVID ALLEN

The Hats on the Table

Marcus loved building things.

When he launched his software company, he knew it would require a lot of him, and at first, he wore every hat with pride.

Sales? Check.

Product development? Check.

Operations, customer service, financial planning, strategic vision? Check, check, check.

For a while, the adrenaline was enough to carry him.

But after two years, the cracks were starting to show.

His product roadmap was slipping.

His sales pipeline wasn't getting the attention it needed.

Financial reporting felt rushed, reactive, more about keeping up than leading ahead.

One weekend, while working late (again), Marcus finally wrote every "hat" he wore on a whiteboard:

- Sales & Marketing
- Product Development
- Financial Management
- Operations
- Customer Support
- Strategic Planning

Seeing it all at once made something obvious: *He* wasn't choosing where to spend his energy, the business was choosing *for* him. He was working with urgency, but not strategy.

Marcus realized he didn't just need to manage his tasks better, he needed to allocate his time as a *founder*, not just a *doer*.

He didn't need to do less important work faster. He needed to decide what tasks only he could do, and focus on them like it was the future of the company.

Because it was.

Let's Reflect on This

Let's step out of the hustle for a moment and look at how you're allocating your energy.

1. What "hats" are you currently wearing in your business?
2. Which of these tasks truly require *your* unique energy, insight, or leadership, and which could eventually be systematized, automated, or delegated?
3. Where are you spending time because it feels easier or immediately urgent, rather than because it's the best use of you?
4. What vital future-focused work (strategy, revenue planning, scaling systems) keeps getting crowded out by urgent operational work?
5. If you could reallocate 10 percent more time toward growth-driving work this month, where would it go?

You are the *founder*, not a jack-of-all-trades.

Owning your role, and protecting your highest-value work, is an act of leadership.

Realign & Move Forward

You can do a lot, but not everything at once. Protect the work that only you can do.

Action Step: Conduct a "Hat Audit" this week.

List all the major functions you touch each week (sales, marketing, ops, financials, customer care, etc.).

Color-code or mark them:

Founder-level work: vision, sales, strategic growth, innovation.
Work to delegate: tasks that could eventually be handed off or systematized.
Energy-draining work: tasks pulling you into reaction mode.

Circle the ones only *you* should handle, and delegate or defer the rest.

Even reallocating **10 to 20% of your time** toward future-focused work can completely shift your trajectory over the next 6 to 12 months.

SIXTEEN

ALLOCATING YOUR BUDGET

"Treat every penny like a sewer cover."

—GEORGE HALAS, FOUNDER OF THE CHICAGO
BEARS

The Budget Balancing Act

Samantha had built a promising SaaS platform for project managers.

Like any founder, she wore a dozen hats. But her biggest challenge wasn't writing code or signing deals, it was deciding how to **spend the limited resources she had**.

Every quarter, the tension resurfaced:

- **Product Development** whispered, "Invest in the platform. Improve onboarding. Fix friction points so customers stay longer and advocate louder."
- **Sales & Marketing** shouted: "Expand reach. Fill the pipeline. If new users don't find us, it doesn't matter how good the product is."

Both sides made good arguments, and both were critical.

Samantha wasn't reckless, she tracked churn rates, customer satisfaction, net promoter scores, and lead-to-close ratios religiously.

Still, even with the numbers, the choices weren't simple.

She realized she couldn't just optimize for "what's urgent today."

She needed a simple framework to help her **fund the future** of the company, not just patch the present.

She asked herself two questions every budgeting cycle:

1. What investment will create more durability?
2. What investment will create more momentum?

Then she would balance the budget intentionally: a certain percentage to **stabilize**, for things like product and service enhancements, and a certain percentage to **accelerate**, for things like growth and customer acquisition.

No longer would she make wild guesses or overreact to the loudest problems.

Samantha didn't always get it perfect.

But by honoring both **strength** and **scale**, she gave her business a stronger foundation, and a longer runway.

Let's Reflect on This

Let's set aside the pressure to be perfect and instead focus on being clear and intentional.

1. What is your company's current priority: creating more stability, more momentum, or both?
2. Where signals are existing customers sending you, either through satisfaction, support tickets, or retention patterns?
3. Which improvement or investment would meaningfully strengthen your business for the next 12 months, not just this quarter?
4. What's at greater risk if delayed: improving your offer, or expanding your reach?
5. If you were protecting the *future you're trying to build*, where would you place your next investment?

Budgeting isn't just solving today's pain points. It's choosing tomorrow's possibilities.

Realign & Move Forward

Build a "Stability versus Growth" Budget Frame

- Identify your discretionary spend for the next quarter.
- Split the budget into two intentional categories:
  - **Stabilize** (for things like product, service quality, and internal systems)

- **Grow** (for things like marketing, sales, and customer acquisition)
- Create a flexible target (for example, 60% Growth and 40% Stability, or flip it) based on where your greatest leverage exists right now.
- Revisit monthly and adjust based on:
  - Customer feedback
  - Cash flow health
- Set strategic milestones (for example, product launch or funding round)

Action: Split your next investment into two buckets: stability and growth. Let the ratio reflect the season your company is in.

SEVENTEEN
HAVING DIFFICULT CONVERSATIONS

"Honest disagreement is often a good sign of progress."

—MAHATMA GANDHI

The Conversation That Changed Everything

Thomas had been feeling uneasy about his lead contractor for months. The deliverables were coming in late, communication was inconsistent, and the tension was starting to bleed into client work.

Still, he said nothing.

Every time he sat down to address it, he talked himself out of it: They've been with me since the beginning. It's not that bad. Confrontation isn't worth the risk.

Instead, he compensated by picking up the slack, softening deadlines, and working longer hours.

Then one day, after a client call went sideways, he felt the pressure snap, not from the work, but from all the words he hadn't said.

That night, he texted a mentor: "I think I've been avoiding a conversation that could've solved this six months ago."

The reply came quickly: "Then have it. The silence is costing you more than the truth ever could."

The next morning, Thomas had the conversation. It was uncomfortable, but it was clarifying. And it led to exactly what was needed: change, accountability, and a rebalanced team.

The relief wasn't just in what he said, it was in **finally saying it**.

Let's Reflect on This

Avoided conversations rarely stay quiet. They leak into your energy, work, and clarity.

We avoid conversations not because we don't care, but because we *do*.

We're afraid of hurting someone, damaging trust, and not being able to "fix it."

But silence doesn't protect relationships, it erodes them slowly, until the gap becomes harder to close.

This question: **What conversation am I not having?** isn't just about confrontation.

It's about choosing clarity over comfort, truth over tension.

Realign & Move Forward

Let's create some space for honesty. This isn't about forcing a hard talk, it's about recognizing what's ready to be said.

1. What relationship or situation in your business feels quietly out of sync?
2. What thoughts or truths are you carrying but haven't spoken aloud?
3. What are you afraid will happen if you speak up? And what might happen if you don't?
4. How might this conversation bring clarity, closeness, or closure?
5. What do you need to remember about yourself before having this conversation?

Having Difficult Conversations

Silence costs more than discomfort. Say what needs to be said, with honesty and care.

Action: Identify one unspoken conversation. Draft what you'd say with support and honesty.

PART 5

KEEP MOVING FORWARD

THE MINDSET OF SUSTAINABLE GROWTH

EIGHTEEN

CONSISTENT FORWARD MOVEMEN‾

"All big things come from small beginnings. The seed of every habit is a single, tiny decision."

—JAMES CLEAR, *ATOMIC HABITS*

The Quiet Expense of Inaction

Derrick had been sitting on a decision for over six months: whether or not to finally niche his consulting firm.

He knew the generalist model was holding him back. His messaging was vague, his proposals were getting passed over for firms with clearer value propositions, and his own enthusiasm was fading.

But niching felt risky. It meant saying no to potential

clients and claiming a direction. Even more, it meant committing to a future he wasn't a hundred percent sure about.

So, he stayed where he was. Tweaking. Waiting. Avoiding.

One day, while updating his CRM, he saw something that stopped him. He had made almost exactly the same revenue as the year before, despite working harder.

That night, he journaled a simple prompt:

What's the cost of staying the same?

The answers poured out:

- Lost clarity
- Stagnant revenue
- Low-energy marketing
- Resentment toward work I don't love
- Lower confidence

From these answers, he found he had been afraid of what change might cost.

But he hadn't looked at what *not changing* was already costing him.

And once he saw it, he couldn't unsee it.

Let's Reflect on This

We're often more afraid of change than we are of stagnation.

But comfort often comes with the cost of lost energy, opportunity, clarity, momentum, and peace of mind.

The question isn't just, "What will this pivot cost me?"

It's also, "What is *not* pivoting costing me already?"

When you factor in the *emotional tax* of staying stuck, the drag, the doubt, the dullness, the cost of change often feels lighter than expected.

This question: **What's the cost of staying the same?** isn't about rushing decisions.

It's about seeing clearly and honoring the truth that doing nothing is still a choice, with consequences.

Realign & Move Forward

Let's stop looking at risk in only one direction. Let's ask what's happening *right now*, not just what could go wrong later.

1. What's one area of your business you've been sitting on, even though part of you knows it needs to change?
2. What story are you telling yourself about why it's safer to delay?
3. What is this inaction costing you, financially, emotionally, creatively?
4. If you keep everything the same for another 6 months, what's likely to happen?
5. What might open up if you took one meaningful, low-pressure step toward change?

Consistent Forward Movement

You don't need a breakthrough, just a rhythm that holds. Keep going, even gently.

Action: Choose one daily or weekly habit that helps you feel in motion. Commit to doing it this month.

NINETEEN
USE INTENTIONAL QUESTIONS TO GROW

"People don't really learn when you tell them something. They don't even really learn when they do something. They start learning . . . only when they have a chance to recall and reflect on what just happened."

—MICHAEL BUNGAY STANIER, *THE COACHING HABIT*

The New Dashboard

Jason was a metrics guy. Every Monday morning, he reviewed dashboards: revenue, churn, leads, retention, and time on site. His business was steady, and his team relied on him to keep it that way.

But something was missing.

The business was growing, but Jason wasn't sure if *he* was.

When he discussed this with his partner, she asked him, "How do you measure what is important to you?"

He didn't have an answer.

Later that evening, he opened his journal and wrote one simple phrase:

"What am I measuring that actually matters?"

Then, he made a new dashboard for himself, in a notebook. Each week he answered the questions:

- Am I proud of how I'm showing up?
- Did I speak the truth, even when it was awkward?
- What did I learn this week?
- What felt heavy, and what felt light?
- Where did I move with clarity instead of fear?

That became his real weekly review.

This didn't replace the business numbers, but worked alongside them.

Jason realized that **questions shape outcomes.** Asking himself the right ones not only made him a better entrepreneur, but a better human.

Let's Reflect on This

Most people chase better answers. But the real growth comes from living with better questions.

You'll change. Your business will change. The world will change.

But when you choose the right questions, they grow with

you. They guide you. They hold you accountable, gently but honestly.

The right questions won't always give you clarity. But they'll give you *access* to clarity, again and again.

This chapter's question: **What questions do I want to live by?** isn't the end.

It's your next beginning.

Realign & Move Forward

Let's close this chapter, and this book, with intention.

1. What question do you return to again and again when things feel unclear?
2. What question would help you show up more honestly in the work you're doing now?
3. What question do you avoid because you already know the answer?
4. What question would guide your decision-making if you trusted yourself more fully?
5. What question do you want to *wake up with* for the next 30 days?

Use Intentional Questions to Grow

Better questions lead to better clarity. Reflection isn't a detour, it's direction.

Action: Pick one intentional question to ask yourself each week. Journal your honest answers.

TWENTY
CRAFTING YOUR OWN QUESTIONS FOR GROWTH

There are many issues we did not cover here that you may need to solve on your entrepreneurial journey. Use the simple but powerful approach provided here to gain clarity in any challenge you may face and get down to the actual issue you need to resolve.

- Identify the core area to focus on: **Is this about vision, strategy, customers, time, team, money, or mindset?**

- Ask yourself, **"What's really going on here, and what do I want to shift in this core area?"** This question grounds you in the present moment and your desired outcome.

- Craft open-ended questions that challenge your assumptions, reveal blind spots, and help you move forward with intention.

There are many tools, frameworks, etc. that you can use, like the Five Whys we introduced in part 4. We find the Five Whys method digs beneath the surface and uncovers the root cause of the issue to support a quick resolution of the actual issue.

Crafting Your Own Questions for Growth

You don't need someone else's blueprint. Let your own questions lead the way.

Action: Create your "**Better Questions Manifesto**." Write 3 to 5 questions that reflect the person, leader, and creator you're becoming. Revisit them monthly. Let them evolve.

CLOSING REFLECTION

THE QUESTIONS WERE NEVER THE DESTINATION

You've reached the end of this book, but not the end of your work.

If anything, you've just found a new kind of clarity, a new compass for your business.

This book wasn't designed to give you a 10-step blueprint or quick-fix plan. It was built to help you pause, reflect, and realign.

It encourages you to ask what's *really* going on beneath the decisions, delays, and dreams.

As you've moved through these questions, I hope you noticed something:

The way forward doesn't always begin with action. Sometimes it begins with awareness, presence, and truth.

You may not remember every chapter. But you'll remember how certain questions made you feel, what they surfaced, and what they shifted inside of you.

And that's what matters most.

Come back to this book when things feel muddy.

Come back when you're growing and want to stay grounded.

Come back when you're tempted to chase what's shiny instead of what's true.

Because your answers will change, but your willingness to ask the right questions will carry you forward, again and again.

AFTERWORD

FROM ONE ENTREPRENEUR TO ANOTHER

This book started as something personal.

I didn't write it because I had all the answers. I wrote it because I needed better questions *for myself*.

As the founder of iLease Management LLC, I've experienced the weight of leading a business, the push for performance, and the quiet internal friction that comes when you're successful *on the surface* but slightly out of sync beneath it.

I started asking questions not to fix myself, but to find myself again inside the work I'd built.

That process gave me more than clarity. It gave me momentum. Integrity. Peace.

And somewhere along the way, I realized I wasn't the only one who needed that.

So if this book gave you space to breathe, think, or feel seen, then I've done my job.

And if it left you with more questions than answers, even better.

Because in the end, *what* you build matters.

But who you become while building it, that changes everything.

Keep asking. Keep listening.

And most importantly, keep coming back to *yourself*.

Leave this book within reach, not for more reading, but for better asking. Because the right question, at the right time, changes everything.

—JOHN MEEDZAN
FOUNDER & MANAGING PARTNER,
iLEASE MANAGEMENT LLC

If this book resonated, I'd love to hear your story.

Connect with me on LinkedIn
https://www.linkedin.com/in/johnmeedzan/

www.ingramcontent.com/pod-product-compliance
Lightning Source LLC
Chambersburg PA
CBHW031445120626
46545CB00006B/2555